PASTA, FRIED RICE, and MATZOH BALLS

Immigrant Cooking in America

by
Loretta Frances Ichord

Illustrated by
Jan Davey Ellis

M MILLBROOK PRESS ❖ MINNEAPOLIS

For my beautiful grandchildren,
Evan, Jack, Hannah, Audrey, and Malin —LFI

For Beatrice Ellis, who knows how to gather a family together,
both in and out of the kitchen — JDE

Text copyright © 2006 by Loretta Frances Ichord
Illustrations copyright © 2006 by Jan Davey Ellis

Millbrook Press
A division of Lerner Publishing Group
241 First Avenue North
Minneapolis, Minnesota 55401 U.S.A.

Website address: www.lernerbooks.com

Library of Congress Cataloging-in-Publication Data

Ichord, Loretta Frances.
  Pasta, fried rice, and matzoh balls : immigrant cooking in America / by Loretta Frances Ichord ;
illustrated by Jan Davey Ellis.
     p. cm.
  Includes bibliographical references and index.
ISBN-13: 978-0-7613-2913-8 (lib. bdg. : alk. paper)
ISBN-10: 0-7613-2913-7 (lib. bdg. : alk. paper)
  1. Diet—United States—History. 2. Food habits—United States—History. 3. Immigrants—United
States—Nutrition. 4. Cookery—United States. I. Ellis, Jan Davey. II. Title.
  TX360.U6I24 2006
  394.1′2′0973—dc22   2004031103

Manufactured in the United States of America
1 2 3 4 5 6 – JR – 11 10 09 08 07 06

Contents

Introduction

Imagine sailing across a rough sea on a ship crowded with people, heading toward a place called America. After weeks of living in cramped conditions, you arrive at a large, busy port. When you get off the ship, people are milling around the wharf, speaking a language you don't understand and eating foods you've never seen before. This is what most immigrants faced when coming to the New World. Until they became used to the customs of their new country, they found great comfort in the recipes and traditions carried over from their homelands.

These cultural gifts of food and tradition have been arriving in the New World since the sixteenth century, when the Spaniards first landed in the 1500s. In later centuries other immigrants journeyed to America to escape their poverty-stricken homelands destroyed by war, disease, or natural disasters. Some simply longed for freedom of religion and a better life for themselves and their families.

Though the immigrants were proud to be new Americans, they were also proud of their own heritages. Many kept their traditional dishes, but added New World ingredients, creating an array of foods to spice up the American diet.

This book is about how the immigrants adapted their heritages to America's rich resources. It begins in 1565 and ends in 1921, when the whole picture of immigration began to change in America. Fear of worsening economic conditions prompted the United States Congress to pass a quota system in 1921 to limit immigration. By 1924 a law was enacted called the Immigration Act of 1924, which expanded the quota to admit northern and western Europeans and exclude most other groups. This caused immigration to slow dramatically. It did not pick up again until the Immigration Act of 1965, which allowed immigrants already in America to bring over their relatives, triggered a second great wave of immigration into the United States.

Many of you will be able to trace your roots back to the immigrants discussed in this book. However, some of you may not find your ethnic group because only the larger, earlier immigrant groups are discussed. In addition, African Americans and their ancestors' culinary traditions are also not mentioned in this book because they are, along with the English settlers, discussed in my earlier book, *Hasty Pudding, Johnnycakes, and Other Good Stuff: Cooking in Colonial America.*

Besides historical information, recipes from several ethnic groups are included in this book, followed by notes about the customs associated with each dish. An appendix at the end of the book will give directions on how to increase amounts for classroom projects. An adult should assist you in preparing these recipes, as some of the techniques require hot or sharp utensils.

So enjoy the great flavors of America's ethnic food heritage!

1 FOOD AND CULTURE WILL CONQUER

The early British settlers helped to establish the American diet by bringing their traditional dishes from England and blending them with New World foods. However, there were other early colonial powers, like the Spanish, French, Dutch, and Swedish, whose cultures and foods also left their mark on the way Americans eat today.

SPANISH IMMIGRANTS ❀ Way back in the sixteenth century, Spanish conquistadors arrived in the New World, establishing the first European settlement in St. Augustine, Florida, in 1565. Other Spanish conquests during that time took place in the Carolinas, Mexico, and eventually what became the states of California, Arizona, Texas, and New Mexico.

The Spaniards who settled in Mexico in the sixteenth century were introduced to chilies, cacti, pumpkin seeds, avocados (called alligator pears), corn, cocoa, tomatoes, beans, and vanilla grown by the Aztecs and the Mayans.

When Spanish soldiers, missionaries, and noblemen ventured up north from Mexico in the early seventeenth and eighteenth centuries to California and present-day New Mexico, they carried a newly acquired taste for hot and spicy foods to these settlements.

In the warm California sun, the Spanish missionaries planted seeds carried from Mexico and their homeland of Spain. The smell of freshly picked chilies, sweet bell peppers, Spanish onions, tomatoes, red beans,

and sweet potatoes filled the mission gardens. Grape vineyards were planted for wine making, table grapes, and raisins. The padres also grew orchards full of citrus fruits, figs, dates, sweet apricots, avocados, and olives to eat in their dishes and to make cooking oils. The Spaniards increased the protein in their diet by becoming the first settlers to have large herds of cattle and raise sheep, goats, and pigs in great numbers.

The dishes the later Spaniards brought with them are very similar to the lightly seasoned fare still eaten in Spain and are not at all like the spicier foods served in Mexico. In fact, if you ask a Spanish-American cook for a tortilla, you will get a thick omelet made with potatoes and onions and cut into wedges to be eaten for a meal or as a tapa (snack). The word *tapa* really means "lid" because the first tapas served in Spain were pieces of bread used to cover wineglasses to keep the flies out.

Other delicious dishes brought over from Spain are paella (a rice dish made with saffron, along with vegetables, seafood, chicken, and pork), gazpacho (cold fresh vegetable soup), creamy custards, and empanadas (fried dough filled with honey, meat, chicken, tuna, or cheese).

But by far the greatest gift the Spaniards gave to the New World was the cultivation of foods so basic to the American diet.

¡Buen provecho! (enjoy the meal)!

FRENCH IMMIGRANTS ✿ It was in Louisiana, especially around the capital of New Orleans (founded in 1718) and the surrounding bayou country, that French culture in America developed its most lasting roots.

Of these French immigrants, the ones who made the biggest cultural impact in Louisiana were the Acadians, who were French Canadians exiled to Louisiana because they refused to swear allegiance to England. After the Acadians (now known as the Cajuns) settled in southern Louisiana, they became known for their peppery one-pot dishes. They used local ingredients like yams, okra, beans, or rice, and fresh or saltwater fish like crawfish, shrimp, oysters, mussels, or eels taken from the Louisiana gulf coast and the bayous. Other local critters and crops used by the Cajuns were frogs, turtles, alligators, ducks, cane syrup, and pecans.

Along with the Cajuns' unique cooking came another famous French-American cuisine known as Creole food. The Creoles are people born in New Orleans with French and Spanish ancestors or a combination of

several ethnic groups of African, Caribbean, French, and Spanish origin. Unlike the Cajuns who made their home in a tough environment, many of the Creole dishes were created on wealthy plantations by French or Spanish chefs and were considered haute cuisine (fancy French cooking).

The famous dishes that came from Cajun and Creole cooks include gumbo (thick soup), jambalaya (a rice dish similar to paella), crawfish pie, and turtle soup. Traditional Cajun cooking uses large amounts of lard (pork fat) and spices. Creole dishes contain more tomatoes, cream, and butter.

So maybe turtle soup, fried frog legs, or alligator sausage won't be making an appearance on your family's dinner table, but you'd be surprised at the many traditional French foods you do eat and think of as everyday American fare. French onion soup, quiche (savory pie), French bread, mayonnaise, French mustards, Roquefort cheese (blue cheese from Roquefort, France), chocolate éclairs, soufflés (a puffy dish made with lots of eggs), and crepes (very thin pancakes) are just a few of the many foods of French origin eaten by Americans.

Bon appétit (good appetite)!

DUTCH IMMIGRANTS ❖ Soon after the Dutch merchants settled in the New World in the early 1600s, many Dutch farmers sailed over from the Netherlands with horses, cattle, sheep, hogs, and poultry. On their ships they also had sacks of seeds and grains for planting wheat, rye, fruit trees, and vegetables. They were not going to be caught without foodstuffs in the winter and starve to death like many of the English settlers in Virginia and New England had done. These Dutch were experts at preserving their meats, vegetables, and fruits by pickling, salting, and drying them.

Probably some of your favorite foods are dishes brought over by Dutch immigrants, like coleslaw, doughnuts, waffles, crullers (twisted sweet cakes deep-fried), and Dutch cocoa.

Goede eetlust (good appetite)!

SWEDISH IMMIGRANTS ❖ In 1638 the first Swedish immigrants established a colony in the New World in

Delaware. They built a small settlement populated by soldiers, traders, and farmers and called it Fort Christina, on the site of present-day Wilmington, Delaware. The area became known as New Sweden, but it was short-lived. The Dutch took it over in 1655, and then the English conquered the whole region in 1664.

Though other Swedish immigrants continued to come to the New World in the 1600s and 1700s, they and the other Scandinavians from Finland, Denmark, Iceland, and Norway made more of an impact on American life when they arrived in a large wave in the nineteenth century. Over a million Swedish immigrants alone came to America between 1850 and the 1920s. Swedish farmers headed for frontier states like Illinois, Minnesota, Iowa, and Wisconsin; ironworkers settled in Massachusetts; miners went to upper Michigan; lumbermen and fishermen moved to the Pacific Northwest and San Francisco.

No matter where the Swedish immigrants settled in America or what they did, like all the other immigrants, no one forgot the recipes and customs of their homeland. One of their charming traditions is the coffee party (*fika*) they hold for friends and family. Alongside their beloved strong coffee, buns, cheese, cakes, and cookies (sometimes seven different kinds) are served. This Swedish custom is responsible for inspiring the modern-day coffee break in America's workday.

In addition to the foods and coffee served at fikas, many Swedish Americans enjoy foods like open-faced sandwiches, cured salmon (gravlax), nettle soup (made from prickly plants called stinging nettles), Swedish pancakes (served at supper, not breakfast), and pea soup.

Var så god (come and eat)!

SWEDISH MEATBALLS
(Swedish-American)

30 small meatballs

You will need:
1/3 cup plain bread crumbs
3/4 cup milk
2 tablespoons finely
  chopped onions
2 tablespoons butter
7 ounces lean ground beef
7 ounces lean ground pork
1 egg, beaten
1 teaspoon salt
1/4 teaspoon white pepper

Equipment:
measuring cups
  and spoons
large mixing bowl
9-inch skillet
wooden spoon
slotted spoon
platter

What to do:
1. Soak bread crumbs in milk for 10 minutes in mixing bowl.
2. In skillet, lightly brown onions in 1 tablespoon butter. Set aside.
3. Add beef and pork to the milk-soaked bread crumbs. Then add onions, egg, salt, and white pepper, mixing well with wooden spoon.
4. Dip hands in cold water before making meatballs. Make each the size of a walnut.
5. Heat remaining tablespoon of butter in skillet.
6. Fry about 6 to 10 meatballs at a time on medium-low heat until meatballs are browned and cooked all the way through. Remove meatballs with slotted spoon and place on platter.
7. Serve with other foods on a smorgasbord, or if it is the main course for a dinner, make meatballs larger and serve with lingonberry preserve (tastes like cranberry sauce), boiled potatoes, and a tossed salad.

Smorgasbord: An Old Swedish Tradition

Köttbullar (Swedish meatballs) in the 1800s were often prepared by Swedish-American pioneers with ground venison, or deer meat, until they could obtain cattle and pigs.

As the pioneers prospered in the New World, these Swedish immigrants began to serve their meatballs on a traditional Swedish buffet table called the smorgasbord. They introduced this dining custom, especially reserved for holiday celebrations, to other Americans at Scandinavian church suppers. The smorgasbord is placed on a large table and consists of a variety of hot and cold foods, including fish dishes (herring is always one of the several kinds of fish served), meatballs (with sauce or without), vegetables, egg dishes, a potato casserole called Jansson's Temptation (made of potatoes, onions, anchovies, and cream), cheese, buns, and crispbreads.

Here are some rules of the smorgasbord:

1. You can return to the smorgasbord as many times as you want, so never load your plate with too many different kinds of foods at the same time.

2. Start with the herring and other smoked, pickled, or poached fish along with a potato dish, crispbread (a crisp flatbread), and some butter.

3. With a clean plate, return for cold cuts and salads.

4. Next try the hot dishes, followed by servings of cheese, fruit, coffee, and fruit drinks.

THE GERMAN AND IRISH IMMIGRANTS
Bring Their Gifts of Food and Tradition

Though the English colonists were the largest European group to settle in early America, the German immigrants were the second biggest, with the Irish coming in a close third. By 1820, when all immigrants were officially counted on passenger arrival lists, the German and Irish presence was steadily growing. By the twentieth century, millions upon millions of German Americans, Irish Americans, and their descendants were living in the United States.

It might surprise you to see how much of German and Irish heritage has become a part of the American culture.

THE GERMAN IMMIGRANTS ❧ Before Germany became a national state in 1871, German folklore and recipes were brought to the New

World by ethnic Germans. They were people who spoke German as their mother tongue and came from a number of German-speaking lands like Austria, Switzerland, parts of Russia, and the Balkan countries.

The first organized group of ethnic Germans arrived in the New World in 1683, after being invited by the English Quaker William Penn to settle in his Pennsylvania colony. These Germans called themselves the Pennsylvania Deutsch (Deutsch meaning "German"). But, somehow, other colonists began calling them the Pennsylvania Dutch, even though the immigrants were not from the Netherlands.

The Pennsylvania Dutch were skilled farmers and cooks who had to adapt to limited food supplies when they first arrived, until they prospered and were able to grow wheat for flour and obtain farm animals to provide milk, butter, meat, and eggs. From their gardens and larders, they made their favorite sour dishes, such as pickled beets, pickled pigs feet, and chowchows (relishes of chopped vegetables in mustard sauce). They balanced their tart foods with sweet dishes like cinnamon apples and baked goods such as shoofly pies (cooks had to "shoo" away flies from the molasses-rich pies cooling on windowsills), funeral pies (raisin pies taken to get-togethers after funerals), kuchen (coffee cakes), sugar cakes, sticky buns, and apple strudel.

The Pennsylvanian Dutch became well known in the middle colonies for their delicious, simple fare and their motto: "Kissin' wears out, cookin' don't."

During the eighteenth and early nineteenth centuries, hundreds of other German immigrants settled in the middle colonies, bringing more traditions like setting up an evergreen tree in the house during Christmas, the brewing of beer, and the introduction of the pretzel. When the colonies became overcrowded, German-American farmers who wanted more land migrated to states like Ohio, Indiana, and Illinois before fanning out to all parts of the Union, including the heart of Texas.

Those immigrants who settled in growing cities and towns started the first delicatessens in the United States (food shops selling cooked meats and prepared salads) and sold German-American favorites, such as frankfurters (also called wieners or dachshund sausages, not named "hot dogs" until 1901), potato salad, sauerkraut (pickled cabbage), sauerbraten (pot roast marinated in vinegar), liverwurst (a liver sausage), Limburger cheese, wiener schnitzel (a thin breaded veal cutlet), and bratwurst (pork sausage).

THE IRISH IMMIGRANTS ❀ In the 1700s many of the Irish in America were mostly from Ulster (now Northern Ireland) and of the Protestant faith. Then in 1820, when Irish Catholics began immigrating to America in an ever-growing stream, the Irish from Ulster began calling themselves Scotch Irish. They did this partly because their ancestors were originally from Scotland before settling in Ireland, but mainly because they wanted to set themselves apart from the incoming Irish immigrants.

By 1847 millions of Irish Catholics were leaving Ireland after a fungus began destroying their potato crops, causing widespread starvation. These desperate Irish sailed to America only to find tough living conditions in overcrowded and dirty urban neighborhoods called shantytowns. They suffered from a great deal of prejudice because they were Catholic, poor, and mostly unskilled.

Despite the hardships, the Irish fell in love with America. And with time, they began to improve their lives, moving out of the ethnic neighborhoods and spreading themselves into all the colonies, but their favorite cities were Boston and New York City. Others worked on the railroads, the Erie Canal, or tried the "luck of the Irish" and rushed to the gold and silver mines in the Far West to find their "pot of gold."

These hardy Irish immigrants gave the New World many gifts from their heritage like Waterford crystal, fine Irish linens, racehorses, shamrocks, the Irish jig, and the folklore of the leprechauns (Irish elves). They also brought their love of salmon, sole (flatfish), prawns, mackerel, and lobster, delighting in being able to catch these same seafoods in the waters off America's eastern and western coasts.

One special memory the Irish carried with them was of their soda bread. In their former homeland, this biscuitlike loaf was baked in a heavy iron pot over a peat (turf from the bog lands of Ireland) fire. Irish cooks believed the peat gave their bread its special flavor. However, in America, the Irish found their bread tasted just fine cooked in an oven or wood fire, as did their Irish stew, oatmeal mush, many potato dishes, and soups.

In addition to everyday fare, corned beef and cabbage is a well-known Irish-American dish eaten traditionally on St. Patrick's Day.

GERMAN POTATO SALAD
(German-American)

6–8 servings

You will need:
10 medium red potatoes
8 bacon slices, chopped
1 red onion, finely chopped
4 teaspoons unbleached all-purpose flour
2 tablespoons sugar
salt and pepper to taste
3/4 cup cider vinegar
1/2 cup water
1/4 cup minced fresh parsley
1 teaspoon celery seeds

Equipment:
large cooking pot
paring knife
large serving bowl
heavy skillet
measuring cups
measuring spoons
wooden spoon

What to do:
1. Place potatoes in cooking pot and cover with water. Bring to a boil, then cook over medium heat until tender. Have an adult drain water out of pot and let potatoes cool slightly.

2. Have an adult help you peel the potatoes with paring knife. Slice thinly and place in serving bowl.

3. Cook bacon in heavy skillet until crisp. Add onion and cook for one minute.

4. Stir in flour and sugar with wooden spoon for one minute. Season with salt and pepper.

5. Slowly mix in vinegar and water and cook until thickened, stirring for about ten minutes.

6. Pour mixture over potatoes. Sprinkle with parsley and celery seeds. Toss lightly and serve warm.

A Traditional German Dish

Potato salad (*Kartoffelsalat*) was first introduced to America by German immigrants. Many versions of this salad are eaten today, but this recipe is the most traditional and never served cold. It is best eaten with bratwurst and plenty of mustard.

Guten appetit (good appetite)!

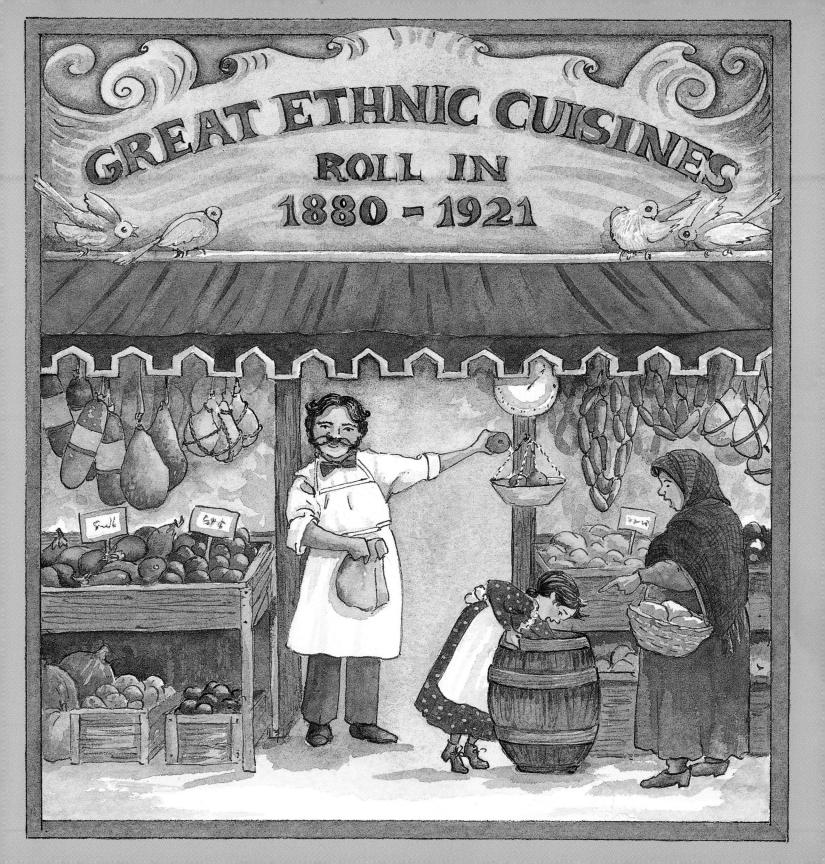

3

ITALIAN IMMIGRANTS

Spicing Up the American Diet

From 1880 to 1920, 23 million immigrants poured into America!

Since many of these immigrants from southern and eastern Europe were poor, didn't speak English, and looked and acted differently, they had to endure much prejudice from native-born Americans. However, many of these foreigners did eventually blend into American society, not by giving up their heritages, but by enriching their new homeland's culture with their Old World traditions and flavorful dishes.

During this great immigration period, the Italians were the largest ethnic group to enter the United States and with them came a rich culinary history. The Italian Americans, more than any other ethnic group, have expanded the American cuisine and had a lasting effect on what Americans love to eat. Pizza pie, anyone?

THE ITALIAN IMMIGRANTS ❀ When the Italian immigrants first reached New York City between the 1880s and early 1900s, many of them stayed in the busy urban area while others scattered to just about every state in the Union. Many Americans had little respect at first for these immigrants from Italy. As a result, no matter where the Italian immigrants settled in America, they formed a "Little Italy," crowding together in one neighborhood with their own restaurants, delicatessens, espresso coffee shops, and food markets.

What part of Italy the immigrants came from determined what culinary traditions they brought with them. If they came from northern Italy, their cooking reflected their love of dairy products, such as butter, cream, and cow's milk cheeses. Cured meats like prosciutto (ham salted and air dried for a year) and spicy sausages were and still are popular in this region. Central Italy's food is heartier, with bean soups and roasted meats. Southern Italians, where many of the peasant stock hailed from, favor olive oil, sheep's milk cheeses, but not as much meat, except for veal (meat from a young calf), and a liking for more seasonal foods, such as tomatoes and fresh herbs used in many seafood dishes.

Gennaro Lombardi, a southern Italian immigrant from Naples, brought over the recipe for pizza and was the first to sell this fragrant pie in America when he opened a pizzeria in New York City in 1905. The pizza dough was kneaded, stretched, and rolled on a marble slab, just like it was done in Italy. Other Italian immigrants and a few daring tourists ate his pizzas. However, pizza didn't really become popular with most Americans until after World War II, when an American businessman featured a pizza maker juggling and throwing pizza dough in the air in front of a shop window. Americans were lured into tasting this tempting flattened bread topped with tomato sauce, cheese, and olive oil, and the rest is history.

Many Italians from all the regions of Italy settled in California, as city dwellers in San Francisco or as truck farmers on the state's fertile lands. They became successful growers of broccoli, eggplants, artichokes (rejected by other growers, until the Italians showed Americans how to prepare and cook them for the best flavor), Savoy cabbage, fava beans, tomatoes, and many other vegetables, nuts and fruits. Large plots of land were devoted to the growing of fresh herbs important to Italian cooking, such as oregano, basil, thyme, fennel, rosemary, sage, parsley, marjoram, and bay leaf. In addition, grape growers developed into famous Italian-American vintners, like the Gallo family.

Besides showing other Americans how to enjoy fresh farm produce, the Italian Americans also demonstrated the many inexpensive and delicious ways to fix their favorite food: pasta! The immigrants from the southern regions of Italy favor rich tomato sauces on their pasta, while the northern Italians prefer less sauce or maybe just some garlic and olive oil. No matter what sauce is on the spaghetti (little strings), fettuccine (small ribbons), linguine (little tongues), penne (quill pens), ravioli (bits and pieces), vermicelli (little worms), or lasagna (ruffled ribbons), pasta should always be cooked al dente (to the teeth). This means cooking pasta until it is still a bit firm and barely tender to the teeth. No soggy pasta, please!

It is important to note that spaghetti and meatballs is strictly an Italian-American dish. This combination does not exist in Italy. If native Italians eat meat with their spaghetti, it is in the form of ground beef or roast cooked with the sauce. Another American pasta invention that native Italians had no hand in creating is cold macaroni salad mixed with mayonnaise. Mama mia, what a way to treat pasta!

It wasn't until 1945, after World War II had ended, that Italian Americans were truly accepted into American society. Their love of life, strong family structure, tantalizing foods, passionate music (especially opera), and deep loyalty to their new country had finally won over other Americans.

So, enjoy all those everyday Italian-American foods you love to eat like pizza, spaghetti, lasagna, garlic bread, green salad with olive oil and vinegar, macaroni, salami, bologna sandwiches, and so much more!

Mangia, mangia (eat, eat!).

GNOCCHI POTATO PASTA

(Italian-American)

4–6 servings

You will need:

2 pounds russet potatoes
2 eggs
1 tablespoon butter
1 tablespoon olive oil
1 teaspoon salt
2 cups unbleached flour
flour for dusting
butter
Parmesan cheese

Equipment:

large cooking pot with lid
small kitchen fork
pot holders
paring knife
potato masher
wooden or plastic board
small mixing bowl
measuring cups and spoons
rolling pin
cookie sheet
slotted spoon
serving bowl

What to do:

1. Place potatoes in cooking pot and fill with water, covering potatoes. Bring to boil. Put lid on pot and lower to medium high. Continue to cook potatoes until tender when tested with fork.

2. Have an adult remove pot from heat with pot holders and carefully drain water. Remove potatoes and pour cold water on them before peeling with paring knife.

3. Place peeled potatoes back in empty pot and mash with potato masher. Put potatoes on board and form into a mound, making a crater in the middle like a volcano.

4. Crack eggs and beat with fork in small mixing bowl.

5. Put beaten eggs, butter, olive oil, and salt in crater. Work the potatoes and egg mixture together with hands. Add flour slowly to potato mixture to form a soft dough.

6. Gather dough into a ball and roll out in a long cylinder on lightly floured board.

7. Cut cylinder crosswise into eight large pieces. Roll each piece into a long 1/2-inch rope. Cut each rope on a diagonal into pieces of dough 3/4 inches long.

8. Roll each piece (gnocchi) off the floured tines of fork and lay on a cookie sheet.

9. Fill the large cooking pot with water again and bring to a boil.

10. Add gnocchi, several at a time, and bring to another boil. When gnocchi rise to the top, scoop out with slotted spoon and place into serving bowl.

11. Any number of tomato or cheese sauces can be added to gnocchi. But butter and Parmesan cheese over these potato dumplings/pasta is also very good.

Serve immediately.

The Traditional Meal: Italian Style

Gnocchi (pronounced nyoh-kee) is a pasta dish that may be eaten as an entrée or as one of the dinner courses of a traditional Italian meal. The first course is the antipasti (the plate before the meal), which may consist of relishes, artichokes, olives, grilled eggplant, red bell peppers with olive oil and garlic, marinated mushrooms, and thin slices of salami. The second course is usually a small bowl of soup like minestrone (thick vegetable soup with beans). The third is a salad (always by itself, not a side dish), but salads may be served at any time during the meal even at the end. Next comes a small plate of pasta with any number of sauces, including tomato, a cheese sauce, or simply olive oil and garlic. The entrée (the main part of meal) will be roasted lamb, roast beef, veal, or fish. The dessert is usually something light like fruit and cheese, but could be something sweeter like biscotti (twice-baked cookies), cream cakes, or cannoli (pastry shells filled with whipped ricotta cheese). Many a belt buckle has to be loosened after such a meal!

EASTERN EUROPEANS
Introduce Great Sausages and Other Delicacies

During the late 1880s, eastern Europeans left their countries of Hungary, Czechoslovakia, Yugoslavia (including Slovenia, Croatia, and Serbia), Lithuania, Romania, Poland, and the Ukraine for a land where they had heard the streets were "paved with gold." They soon found that the streets of America were not golden and many not paved at all.

Nonetheless, thousands of these immigrants stayed, living in crowded tenements (run-down apartment buildings with small windowless rooms) close to factories where they worked. Since there was no refrigeration in their cramped quarters and supermarkets were not even imagined, getting food for the table was a daily chore. Children were often sent to shop for a loaf of bread at the bakery, a piece of fish from the fishmonger, milk from the dairyman, meat, pork, or lamb from the local butcher shop, and vegetables from the greengrocer's produce stalls. Many immigrants tried new foods and included them in their treasured recipes. For some it was a delight to take their first taste of a fresh tomato, an orange, a banana, or a crisp lettuce leaf.

As these new Americans prospered, they moved away from the crowded neighborhoods in which they lived with their fellow country-men, making room for the next group of newly arrived immi-grants. They began to assimilate (blend in with the general popu-lation) and live in better housing where they could afford to eat their favorite dishes and desserts any time during the year and not just on holidays.

Of all the eastern European immigrants, Americans have borrowed most food ideas and recipes from the Hungarians and the Polish.

HUNGARIAN IMMIGRANTS ❖ Most of the people of Hungary are Magyars, descendants of Finno-Ugric and Turkish tribes who lived with Avar and Slavic people in Hungary during the ninth century. Now almost two million Americans claim to have Hungarian (Magyar) ancestors who immigrated to America in the late 1800s and early 1900s. The social, political, and economical unrest that occurred after the Austro-Hungarian Empire (Austria and Hungry became dual monarchies under one ruler in 1867) fell in 1918, caused many Hungarians to flee their country and sail to America.

Besides contributing to the sciences and other important industries, Hungarian immigrants brought the flavors of Hungary to America. They believed and still do, that love, music, and food are the three most impor-tant things to make one happy and content in life. The drinking of good

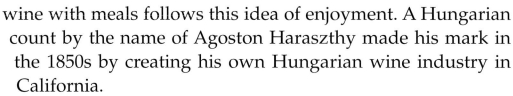

wine with meals follows this idea of enjoyment. A Hungarian count by the name of Agoston Haraszthy made his mark in the 1850s by creating his own Hungarian wine industry in California.

When it comes to food, the Hungarian Americans are talented cooks, baking delicate strudels (layers of paper-thin pastry), walnut coffee cakes, butter cookies, and doughnuts with prune-butter centers. The American cuisine adopted Hungarian-inspired dishes like chicken paprika, stuffed peppers, stuffed cabbage rolls, noodles, soups, and Hungarian goulash, or *gulyas* (a famous stew made of beef, potatoes, carrots, and tender dumplings cooked with lard, paprika, and onions). This hearty dish dates back to the ninth century when the Magyars (Hungarians) were still nomadic tribes and cooked over open fires with large kettles.

Hungarian-American cooks are never without paprika, an important flavoring in many of their dishes. If you look on your family's spice shelf in the kitchen, you will probably find a small can or bottle of this orange-colored spice, as it is a popular flavoring used in many American dishes. Paprika comes from grinding the dried pods of a certain variety of pepper that has lots of zip, but it is not overly hot. The Hungarian Americans call their much-loved paprika a "sweet and noble rose."

POLISH IMMIGRANTS ❖ The Polish who came to America in the late 1880s and early 1900s were the third largest immigrant group to enter next to the Italians and the Jews. From 1795 to 1919, no Polish state existed, so the ethnic Poles who came to America in the nineteenth century were mainly from the German, Austro-Hungarian, and Russian empires. When they arrived on America's shores, the Polish immigrants found New York, New Jersey, Pennsylvania, the Great Lakes region, and southern New England to their liking.

Maybe some Polish-American foods like a relish of beets and horse-radish might take some getting use to, but the one food the Polish immigrants brought over with them that many Americans have come to love is the Polish sausage (kielbasa). Garlic-flavored pork, studded in shiny casings, hang in butcher shops, delicatessens, and stack neatly in wrapped packages at local supermarkets all over America. They are the greatest culinary contribution from the Polish-American community.

BABKA EASTER YEAST CAKE
(Polish-American)

8–10 servings

You will need:
1 packet of active dry yeast
1 cup sugar
3 eggs
3/4 cup butter
1 cup milk
3 cups unbleached flour
1 teaspoon grated orange rind
1 teaspoon grated lemon rind
1 teaspoon vanilla extract
1/2 cup raisins,
    presoaked in hot water and drained
cooking spray

Glaze:
2/3 cup powdered sugar
1 tablespoon lemon juice
1 tablespoon orange juice

Equipment:
large mixing bowl
wooden spoon
dinner fork
small mixing bowl
measuring cups and spoons
small saucepan
bundt pan
rubber spatula
kitchen towel
toothpick
pot holders
large plate

What to do:

1. Mix yeast and sugar together in large mixing bowl with wooden spoon. Beat eggs in small mixing bowl with fork before adding to yeast and sugar.

2. Heat milk and butter in saucepan on medium heat until butter is melted. Add to yeast mixture along with flour, grated orange and lemon rind, vanilla, and raisins. Mix well with wooden spoon.

3. Grease bundt pan with cooking spray. Fill pan with batter, using rubber spatula. Cover pan with towel and let stand in warm place until doubled in size (about 2 hours).

4. Preheat oven to 325° F. Bake cake about 1 hour or when a toothpick is poked into cake and comes out clean.

5. Have an adult remove pan with pot holders and let cool for 10 minutes.

6. Turn pan upside down over a plate and remove cake.

7. Mix with fork the powdered sugar, lemon and orange juices in washed small mixing bowl until smooth. Pour glaze over top of cake.

8. Slice cake and serve. Very good!

The Polish Tradition of Easter Eve

Most Polish Americans are devout Catholics who center their favorite foods about religious holidays. None is more important to them than Easter and the Swieconka (pronounced shveeyen-tson-kah) ceremony. This is the very old tradition of blessing food the Saturday before Easter. Baskets with white cloths are filled with a sampling of foods to be eaten on Easter Sunday and taken to church on Easter Eve to be blessed by the parish priest. The baskets contain traditional foods like butter (shaped into a lamb), sausage, salt, cheese, horseradish, rye bread, a slice of Babka (means grandmother in Polish), sausage, ham, smoked bacon, and decorated hard-boiled eggs. The hard-boiled eggs are the most important symbol to the Polish, meaning new life. On Easter day, before the real feast begins, the blessed hard-boiled eggs are shared with family members to wish them good health and happiness.

5

JEWISH IMMIGRANTS
Special Culinary Traditions

Do you like to nosh on knishes? If you do, than you enjoy snacking on a Jewish-American pastry filled with potatoes, meat, or cheese. If you haven't tried knishes, how about a slice of cheesecake, a hot pastrami sandwich on rye bread, a kosher pickle, or a bagel with cream cheese? Many of the above foods stem from Jewish religious practices that have crossed over into non-Jewish kitchens. When the first Jewish immigrants arrived with their cooking pots, candlesticks, and beloved recipes, they created a major center of Jewish cultural and culinary traditions in America.

JEWISH IMMIGRANTS ❁ The earliest Jewish immigrants to arrive in the New World settled in New Amsterdam (now known as New York) in 1654. They were Sephardic Jews who came from Spain, Portugal, North

Africa, Greece, Turkey, the Middle East, and other countries of the Mediterranean region. It was mainly the Sephardic Jews who were the first to establish a center for Judaism in America with their cuisine and many synagogues on the East Coast.

While these early Jewish immigrants ate like other colonists at the time, using corn, beans, and other fresh foods in their dishes, they did introduce a new way of frying foods by using olive oil instead of lard.

After 1830, Ashkenazic Jews from German-speaking lands and eastern Europe arrived in America with their Yiddish language (based on German and Hebrew) and traditions. Many of these Jewish immigrants adapted their dishes to what was available regionally. The Jews in the southern states of Mississippi and Alabama put pecans in their tortes and cookies, instead of almonds. In Louisiana, they spiced up their matzoh balls with hot peppers and scallions. In Ohio, molasses and brown sugar were used in recipes instead of honey, and in Washington State, Jews chose salmon over carp for Sabbath celebrations.

During the great immigrant wave of 1880, millions more Ashkenazic Jews arrived in America after escaping persecution in their homelands. In the New World they hoped to find "the land of milk and honey," where comfort, sweetness, and peace awaited them. Most American Jews are descendents of these Ashkenazic Jews.

The Jewish immigrants faced the same challenges of any new settlers, but unlike other newcomers, the Jews had a unique problem, how to observe the laws of *kashrut* (Jewish dietary laws of cleanliness) in their new homeland. To obey these laws, foods must be kosher (pure and fit according to Jewish ritual). The Jewish pioneers traveling out West had an especially hard time finding kosher foods. To avoid eating *treif* foods (forbidden and not kosher), many consumed a limited diet of vegetables and grains until they could establish a Jewish community.

What are kosher foods and how do the laws of *kashrut* work? The following is a list of these rules:

1. Certain animals cannot be eaten, such as those creatures who do not have cloven hooves and do not chew their cuds. The camel, rock badger, the hare, and the pig are nonkosher. Sheep, cattle, goats, and deer are kosher.

2. Any fish with scales and fins may be eaten including tuna, carp, salmon, and herring. Shellfish such as lobster, oysters, shrimp, clams, and crabs are all forbidden.

3. Birds of prey or scavengers are not permitted. Chicken, geese, ducks, and turkeys are allowed.

4. Animals are only kosher if slaughtered by Jewish law in a ritual called *shechitah* and by a person called a *shochet*. The method has to be a quick deep stroke across the throat with a sharp blade. Most of the blood must be drained from the animal. The remaining blood is removed either by broiling or soaking and salting. All must be done within seventy-two hours of slaughter.

5. Meat cannot be eaten with dairy. However, fish, eggs, fruits, vegetables, and grains can be eaten with either meat or dairy meals and are called *pareve* (neutral food).

By the early 1900s, many Jewish-American foods became processed and labeled with trademarks, indicating the food to be kosher. The most well known of the over 120 of these symbols is the letter *U* inside a circle on a food label. It stands for the Union of Orthodox Jewish Congregations, confirming that the product has been inspected by a group of rabbis and deemed to be in compliance with Jewish dietary laws.

Not all religious Jewish Americans keep kosher, but many do to some degree or another. Numerous Jewish Americans also celebrate Shabbat (Sabbath), which starts every Friday afternoon and lasts until after sundown on Saturday. This is a time for relaxation, attending religious services, lighting candles, and being with family and friends. It is also a time for enjoying festive foods like challah (a sweet bread shaped into a braid), gelfite fish (stewed or baked fish mixed with matzoh crumbs, eggs, and seasonings and shaped into balls or oval cakes), cholent (a slow-cooked stew), and, of course, chicken soup. All these dishes are made ahead of time (no cooking, baking, or shopping are allowed during Sabbath).

MATZOH BALLS AND CHICKEN SOUP
(Jewish-American)

Serves 6

You will need for chicken soup:
1 5-pound chicken
2 celery stalks, chopped
1 large carrot, cut into chunks
1 onion, cut into quarters
4 sprigs of parsley
4 sprigs fresh dill
salt and pepper to taste

You will need for matzoh balls:
2 eggs
2 tablespoons canola oil
1 packet from box of matzoh ball mix
1 1/2 teaspoons salt

Equipment:
large soup pot with lid
wooden spoon
measuring cups and spoons
pot holders
large strainer
large deep bowl
small mixing bowl
kitchen fork
4-quart pot
slotted spoon

What to do:

1. Remove giblets from chicken and wash chicken before placing in large soup pot. Fill pot with enough water to cover chicken.

2. Have an adult place pot on stove over high heat. When water starts to boil, skim foam off the top with wooden spoon.

3. Add rest of ingredients, lowering the heat to simmer, and covering the pot. Slow cook for one hour or until chicken is well cooked and falls off bone. Using pot holders, have adult pour hot soup through the strainer into large bowl, ending up with a clear broth.

4. Let broth cool and skim off fat. Put aside.

5. In small mixing bowl whisk with fork 2 eggs and 2 tablespoons oil. Add 1 packet from box of matzoh ball mix, stirring well.

6. Place bowl in refrigerator for 20 minutes.

7. Fill a 4-quart pot halfway up with water, add salt. Put on medium high and bring to boil.

8. Wet hands with water before shaping chilled batter into balls about the size of walnuts.

9. Drop balls into boiling water, cover, and reduce heat, simmer for 20 minutes.

10. Pour chicken broth back into large pot and heat.

11. Remove matzoh balls with slotted spoon from water and drop into broth, simmer together over medium low.

12. Serve hot. L'Chaim (eat well)!

The Jewish Passover Celebration

Matzoh balls and chicken soup are two of the many traditional dishes served during Passover, the most widely observed Jewish holiday. This eight-day festival begins every year on the fifteenth day of the Jewish month of Nissan, falling in either March or April, depending on the English calendar. The Jews call this ancient festival Passover because God passed over their ancestors' homes when the first-born children were slain in Egypt over three thousand years ago.

Before Passover begins, homes are scrubbed inside and out, including all cooking pots and utensils. In addition, all traces of leavened (raised) bread are removed from the house. This is done because when the Israelites (Jewish slaves) escaped from Egypt, they couldn't wait for their bread to rise, so they carried unleavened matzoh (looks like a large flat cracker) with them.

On the first two nights of Passover, the Seder (festive meal) is celebrated with symbolic foods, songs, and customs. During this event, children and adults listen to the reading of the *Haggadah*, a retelling of the Exodus of the Israelites from Egypt during the reign of Pharaoh Ramses II.

6

OTHER ETHNIC GROUPS

Adding Unique Fare

What of the other immigrants who entered America in smaller numbers in the late nineteenth century and established their own ethnic communities and culinary traditions? Among these groups were the Greeks and the Portuguese.

PORTUGUESE IMMIGRANTS ❀ The Portuguese immigrants and their traditions settled in several regions of America, including New England. Many of those from the Azores (nine volcanic islands off the coast of Europe belonging to Portugal) began arriving in California on whaling ships in the 1800s. They continued to come into this western state up into the 1970s.

The Portuguese Americans, who are spread out on farms and dairies up and down the Central Valley of California, come together in the spring and fall for celebrations called festas (non-Portuguese are very welcome).

One of the more famous of these festas is the celebration of the Holy Spirit where *sopas e carne* (thick meat soup) is served to all who attend the event. The festa begins with the queen (a different Portuguese-American girl is selected each year) and her attendants leading a procession from the parish hall to their Catholic church to attend Mass. After the mass, a meal is served featuring large metal bowls containing chunks of bread soaking in a rich cooking liquid and set on the tables. Next come smaller bowls full of sliced pot roast and cabbage flavored with onions, lots of chopped mint, allspice, and garlic.

Besides the tradition of the festa, the Portuguese immigrants also brought other great foods to America, like *lingüica* (spicy pork sausages), kale and potato soup, and meringue cookies so light the Portuguese call them *suspiros* (sighs).

Bom apetite! (Good appetite!).

PORTUGESE SWEET BREAD
(Portuguese-American)

Makes two 9-inch loaves

You will need:
1/4 cup lukewarm water (110°F to 115°F)
1 package dry yeast
a pinch plus 1 1/4 cups sugar
6 cups unbleached flour
1 teaspoon salt
1 cup lukewarm milk (110°F to 115°F)
3 eggs
1 1/2 cups soft butter (3 sticks)
1 teaspoon lemon zest (grated lemon rind)
butter for greasing
flour for dusting
2 tablespoons softened butter
1 egg, slightly beaten

Equipment:
measuring cups
measuring spoons
small bowl
wooden spoon
large mixing bowl
lightly floured wooden
   or plastic board
pastry brush
dish towel
2 9-inch pie plates
2 pot holders
small kitchen knife
2 cake racks

What to do:
1. Pour the lukewarm water in small bowl and sprinkle yeast and a pinch of sugar over it. Let mixture sit for 3 minutes, and then stir to dissolve yeast. Set bowl in a warm place, free of drafts, for 8 minutes or until the mixture doubles in size.

2. In large mixing bowl, combine 1 1/4 cups sugar, 3 1/2 cups of the flour, and salt. Make a hole in the center and pour in yeast mixture, warm milk, and eggs. Gently stir with wooden spoon, and then beat together until all ingredients are well combined.

3. Mix in 3 sticks of butter and lemon zest. Add the remaining 2 1/2 cups of flour, blending in 1/4 cup of flour at a time until dough can be gathered with hands into a soft ball.

4. Place dough on lightly floured board and knead with heels of hands, pressing and pushing forward until dough is smooth and elastic.

5. Wash out large bowl and grease with butter, using the pastry brush. Shape dough into a ball and place in bowl. Dust with a bit of flour before draping a dish towel over dough. Set it in a warm place for 1 to 2 hours or until the dough doubles in size.

6. With pastry brush, coat the bottom and sides of pie plates with 2 tablespoons of softened butter.

7. Remove towel and punch dough down with fist. Take out of bowl and place back on floured board, letting it rest for 10 minutes.

8. Divide dough in half, shaping each half into round loaves and placing them in the pie plates. Let rise for 1 hour.

9. Preheat oven to 350°F degrees.

10. With pastry brush, coat the top of each loaf with beaten egg.

11. Bake both loaves in middle of oven for 30 to 40 minutes or until tops are golden brown and crusty.

12. Have adult remove from oven with pot holders and loosen from pie plates with knife before taking loaves out to cool on cake racks. Slice, eating as is or with butter.

Traditional Portuguese Sweet Bread

Portuguese sweet bread (*Massa Sovada*) is traditionally given out to family and friends in Portuguese-American communities during the Easter holiday. A popular custom during this spring holiday is to put a hard-boiled egg in the middle of the bread to symbolize the continuance of life and the promise of survival.

GREEK IMMIGRANTS ❀ Though the first Greek immigrants arrived in America during the eighteenth century, most came during the great immigrant wave in the late 1800s. As did other ethnic groups before them, they brought along a strong cultural tie with their church. They built Greek Orthodox churches where they settled in California, the Northeast and the North Central section of the United States.

Many Greek immigrants found a new trade in America by opening up restaurants. But, unlike the Italian immigrants, the Greek immigrants didn't serve their own ethnic foods. Their menu consisted of low-priced, general food selections.

It wasn't until air travel allowed Americans to visit Greece that they were able to enjoy Greek foods like moussaka (eggplant layered with minced lamb, seasonings, and thick custard) and Greek salads made with feta cheese (crumbly white goat cheese packed in brine), olives, tomatoes, fresh lettuce, cucumbers, onions, oregano, and drizzled with olive oil and lemon juice (the essence of all Greek cooking).

Annual festivals held at Greek Orthodox churches have also become a popular way for Americans to sample Greek food, watch and listen to the native songs and dances, and see the national costumes of Greece. Some only attend for a taste of the rich Greek dessert called baklava (pastry filled with nuts and soaked in a honey syrup).

Kalli orexi! (Good appetite!).

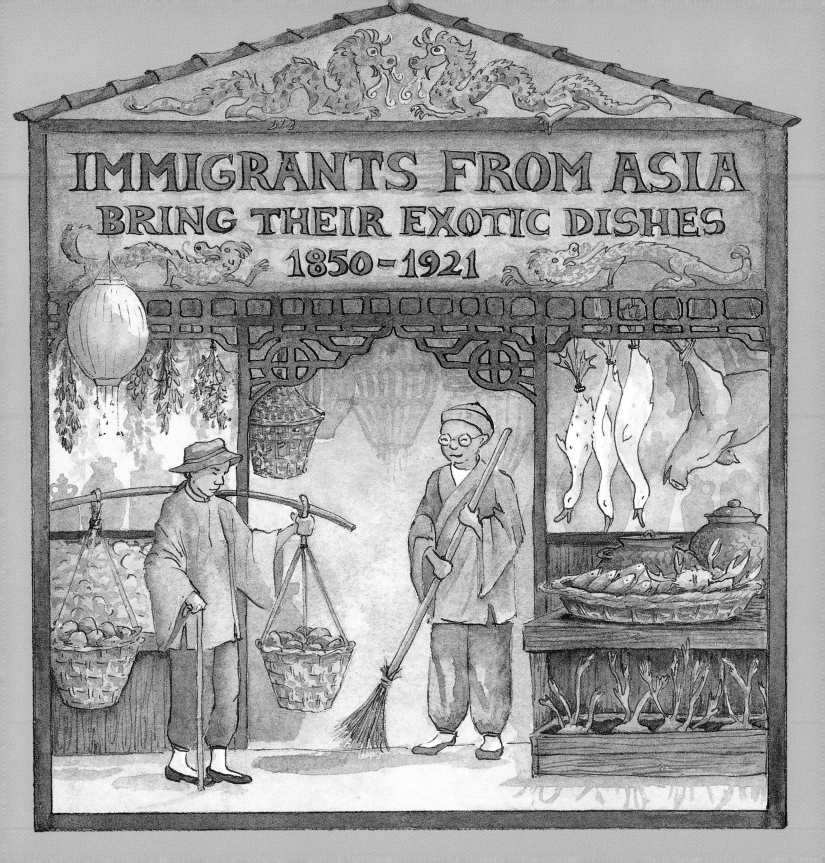

CHINESE IMMIGRANTS
Cooks of Fragrant Cuisine

Many Americans think eating Chinese-American food at home, in a restaurant, or from take-out cartons filled with chow mein, sweet and sour pork, fried prawns, egg foo yung, and crisp fortune cookies is a real treat. But did you know that in the nineteenth and early twentieth centuries many Americans knew little about the Chinese immigrants and their ancient culinary traditions? Despite the great dishes of China we have come to love, it wasn't until after World War II that Chinese Americans were finally looked upon with respect and their foods widely eaten.

CHINESE IMMIGRANTS ❈ All immigrants in America experienced prejudice in one degree or another, but the Chinese, who were the first Asians to come to the United States in the 1850s, suffered from a most severe and punishing form of this discrimination.

Many of the early Asian immigrants were called "sojourners" because they were single males who had come to America to make money and then return to their homeland. Though members of other ethnic groups had done the same thing, when the Chinese did it, greater fuel was added to the prejudicial fire because Americans were afraid the Chinese were taking too much money out of the country. Others feared they would not get jobs because the Asians were willing to work for lower wages (more than

they were making in China). So intense was the hatred for the Chinese that a law was enacted in 1882 called The Chinese Exclusion Act, banning the Chinese from immigrating to the United States unless they had an American-born relative. From 1882 to 1943, when the law was finally repealed, no Chinese were allowed to become a United States citizen.

Despite all this harsh treatment, many Chinese immigrants decided to stay in America because of choice or necessity. However, since they were not accepted into American society, the Chinese immigrants created their own communities called Chinatowns. The biggest of these overcrowded slums were built in San Francisco and New York City, where even the rich Chinese immigrants resided. Chinatowns were and still are the centers of business, shopping, and meeting places for this Asian group. Though in present times, the vast majority of Chinese Americans are no longer tied to Chinatowns and live in neighborhoods with other Americans, some still prefer to stay and work in these communities.

Since food and its careful preparation is such an important part of the Chinese culture, the food business became the biggest source of jobs for newcomers. Restaurants were built on every street corner, serving Cantonese food (most of the early Chinese immigrants came from the southern region of Canton) to other Chinese. In an effort to attract more non-Chinese patrons to their food establishments, Chinese cooks served fried steak and also created a dish called chop suey (odds and ends), con-

sisting of a small amount of pork sautéed with lots of vegetables. So by the early 1900s, a few non-Chinese Americans came to love the delicious and cheap meals offered in these Chinatown eateries.

Though there are Chinatowns scattered in various regions of America, by far the most ethnic and largest is the one in San Francisco, California. It is the Chinese food center of America. If you were to walk the narrow streets of this Chinatown, you would see glazed roasted ducks, crackly skinned roasted pigs, bean curd cakes, and fish tanks with live fish and shellfish in many shop windows and door-ways. Vegetable and fruit stands are every-where and so is the smell of panfried noodles and steaming rice.

By the 1960s, Americans began to discover other regional Chinese cooking other than Cantonese. With new immi-grants arriving, peppery foods from the western province of Sichuan brought dishes with "tingle and sting." Those from the eastern area of Shanghai brought stewed meat and seafood dishes with a liberal use of soy sauce. Northern Chinese immigrants brought Peking duck and spring rolls.

In addition to introducing great flavors, the Chinese Americans have taught other Americans how to use a wok (all-purpose stir-fry pan) to cook vegetables the Chinese way, crisp, not soggy or overcooked, and to enjoy fine Chinese teas.

FRIED RICE
(Chinese-American)

Serves 6

You will need:

1 tablespoon soy sauce
2 eggs, beaten
2 tablespoons vegetable oil
1/2 cup minced onion
1 tablespoon fresh ginger, peeled and minced
1 cup diced cooked ham
4 cups cold, cooked long-grain white rice
1/2 cups peas, frozen or fresh
soy sauce
1/4 cup chopped green onions
sesame oil
white pepper to taste

Equipment:

measuring cups and
    spoons
wok or heavy skillet
wooden spoon
platter

What to do:

1. Add 1 tablespoon soy sauce to beaten eggs. Set aside.

2. Heat wok or skillet to high heat with vegetable oil. When hot, have an adult add onions and ginger. Stir-fry (constantly stir and toss) for about 15 seconds.

3. Add ham and continue to stir-fry for 3 minutes.

4. Add rice and cook over high heat for 2 more minutes.

5. Pour eggs over rice, mixing and stirring for another minute.

6. Add peas and continue to cook for 40 seconds while adding more soy sauce, if needed.

7. Have an adult remove skillet or wok from heat and pour rice on platter.

8. Top with green onions and sprinkle lightly with sesame oil and white pepper.

9. Serve in bowls and eat with chopsticks.

The Tradition of Rice and Chopsticks

Fried rice is a practical everyday dish using leftover rice. Chinese Americans also cook their cherished staple by steaming it, putting it in a casserole, toasting it, or making it into a thin soup called Jook. Since rice is a bland food, it blends in with the flavor of whatever food it accompanies.

A bowl of rice symbolizes all food in Chinese culture and is so important that instead of greeting a person by asking, "How are you today?" a more traditional Chinese greeting would be, "Have you had your rice today?" The proper reply, regardless if the greeted person just had a bowl of rice or hasn't eaten for days, would be, "Yes, I have partaken of sufficiently, thank you."

Chopsticks are the utensils of choice for many Asian Americans when eating their rice and other traditional foods. Using chopsticks takes practice, and the technique is as follows: Hold the first (lower) chopstick in the valley between your thumb and index finger and braced against your third. Hold second (upper) stick as you would a pen. Use thumb and index finger to move upper stick up and down while lower stick remains stationary. It is okay to hold the bowl close to the mouth with one hand while eating the rice with chopsticks in the other, but there are certain etiquette no-no's regarding eating with these utensils:

1. Don't point with chopsticks.
2. Don't fish around in your food with them.
3. Don't lick the sticks.
4. Don't poke your food with the sticks.
5. Don't pretend your stick is a flag and plant it in the middle of your food.
6. Don't wave your chopsticks in someone's face.

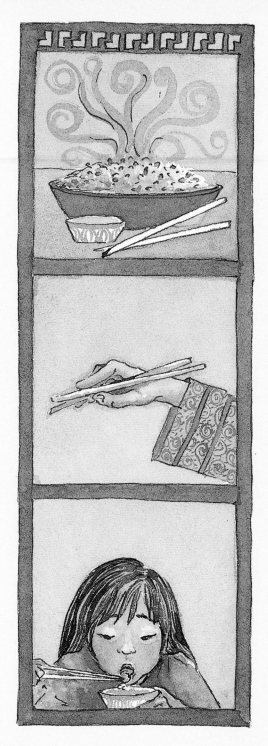

8

JAPANESE IMMIGRANTS

Prepare Food Pleasing to the Eye and the Stomach

Do you like to eat sushi and do karate kicks? Not at the same time of course! These are just a couple of the many traditions that came with the Japanese immigrants when they arrived in America during the 1890s. Though the Japanese and their finely made cars, computers, martial arts, and array of exotic foods are now popular in America, it wasn't always so.

JAPANESE IMMIGRANTS ✿ Most Japanese immigrants in the 1860s worked on Hawaii's sugar plantations. Then, by 1890, they were invited by American companies to work on railroads, sawmills, fish canneries, and mines in the Pacific Northwest and Alaska. They were also recruited to work on California farms where they eventually prospered and bought their own land, growing large crops of fresh green vegetables and strawberries.

However, it was not easy for the Japanese immigrants in America. Like the Chinese, the Japanese in the late nineteenth and early twentieth centuries were labeled the "yellow peril" because the American white society distrusted them. Non-Japanese didn't want these Issei (Japanese immigrants born in Japan and living in America) taking over the job market. Many also feared the ever-increasing might of Japan's military power.

Times became very hard for the Issei and their Nisei (second-generation) children when World War II broke out in 1941 between America and Japan. All Japanese Americans were suspected of helping Japan and were sent to detention camps in the western part of the United States until the war was over in 1945. The Japanese were not allowed to become citizens of the United States until the Immigration and Nationality Act of 1952 was enacted.

When the Japanese Americans finally gained respect in the early 1950s, they began to share with other Americans the traditional dishes they had been enjoying in the privacy of their own homes. Most Americans had not been exposed to Japanese food because there were few Japanese restaurants in the United States before the 1950s. After that time, a crop of Japanese-American eateries appeared on the scene, serving tempura (shrimp and vegetables deep-fried in a light batter), meat and vegetable meals cooked right in front of customers, or exotic sushi (vinegared rice) and raw fish dishes.

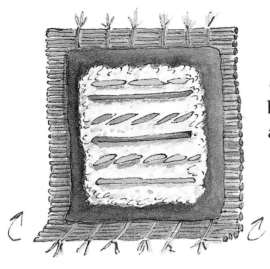

Japanese food is based on what vegetables and fruits are in season, only the best quality of beef and chicken, and what comes from the sea. The Japanese also believe a meal should be displayed in an artistic manner and "a feast to the eye as well as the stomach." For example, vegetables and fruits are often cut into flower shapes before serving.

Since Japan is a series of islands surrounded by the vast Pacific Ocean, many of the ingredients used in Japanese cuisine come from the sea, including seaweed (wild plants grown in underwater fields). The Japanese people believe eating seaweed will make their hair thick, black, and healthy. One popular variety of seaweed called nori (seaweed formed into flat greenish-black papers) is often used to fix a sushi dish called *norimaki*. Sushi is spread out on the nori which has been placed on a small bamboo mat. Fillings like cucumbers, avocados (a California addition), mushrooms, and *wasabi* (horseradish paste—very hot!) are placed on the sushi. Then using the mat, the sushi-laden nori is rolled in jelly-roll fashion. The roll is cut into eight or nine pieces before serving. Another variety of seaweed, *dashi-konbu,* is used to make dashi stock (liquid), which is a key ingredient in many Japanese dishes.

The eating of *sashimi* (raw fish) may seem weird to some westerners, but many Americans have come to love this traditional Japanese dish served at restaurants and food shops. The sashimi must be so fresh that in some Japanese-American restaurants, wiggling sea breams, tunas, lobsters, prawns, or shrimps are pulled from fish tanks, sliced, and served immediately.

Though sake (rice wine) is a popular Japanese hot beverage to drink with meals and an ingredient for dipping sauces, tea drinking has a special place in Asian culture. Japanese tea gardens, like the famous one in San Francisco's Golden Gate Park, are quiet places with ponds, beautiful cherry trees, cedars, dwarf pines, Japanese maples, and winding paths for strolling to the teahouse, where tea and cookies are served.

Tea is also served in Japanese-American homes for guests with great respect and appreciation. To perform a Japanese tea ceremony properly takes years of practice and experience.

SUKIYAKI
(Japanese-American)

4–6 servings

You will need:
2 pounds of sirloin steak
　　frozen for 20 minutes
1 block firm tofu
10 shiitake mushrooms
3 leeks or Japanese long onions
1 Chinese cabbage
1 8-ounce can sliced
　　bamboo shoots
vegetable oil
1 bottle sukiyaki sauce

Equipment:
sharp kitchen knife for slicing
cutting board
2 large platters
large electric griddle
long tongs
wooden scraper
small bowls for serving
chopsticks

What to do:
1. Get steak out of freezer and with an adult's help slice into very thin bite-size slices.
2. Cut tofu into small squares.
3. Slice mushrooms, leeks, and cabbage.
4. Open can of bamboo shoots and drain.
5. Using tongs, arrange sliced food, including bamboo shoots on the two platters, making neat piles of each food. Place platters next to electric griddle in the middle of table.
6. Have everyone sit at table and begin cooking.
7. First coat griddle with vegetable oil and put on high. Fry meat first. Pour some sukiyaki sauce over the meat while cooking. With wooden scraper, move cooked meat to the side of skillet. Cook tofu and mushrooms, moving them to the side when done.
8. Coat the griddle with more oil and pour more sauce on top of food while cooking bamboo shoots, leeks, and cabbage.

9. Have guests take a serving of hot food with their chopsticks and place in their own serving bowls. Eat with the chopsticks.

10. You can add shirataki (arrowroot noodles) and other vegetables like spinach or edible chrysanthemum leaves to a sukiyaki dish. It is okay to make up your own sukiyaki recipe.

11. Hot boiled rice is often served with sukiyaki.

Japanese-American "Friendship Dish"

Sukiyaki is the most popular of Japanese-American nabemono (foods cooked at the table) dishes. It is an easy and fun meal to cook at home for guests or to eat at Japanese restaurants where everyone sits around a large square table with a hot metal grill in the middle as a chef cooks their meal in front of them.

At home many Japanese-American families have their own special recipe for fixing this traditional one-pot dish called the "friendship dish." The more traditional way to have sukiyaki is to dip the hot food into a bowl of beaten raw eggs before eating (may be unsafe and not recommended).

After a final bite of this meal, a piece of fruit or maybe a dish of ice cream might be served. Popular Japanese flavors that could make their way to America are: octopus ice cream, sea urchin ice cream, sea slugs ice cream, and shrimp ice cream. Seconds, anyone?

APPENDIX

Additional directions for using recipes in a classroom with your teacher and thirty-two students

Chapter 1

Swedish Meatballs: Equipment needed: electric frying pan, small paper plates, and plastic forks.

Increase ingredients: Double recipe and make meatballs smaller.

Chapter 2

German Potato Salad: Equipment needed: electric frying pan, portable electric burner to boil potatoes in pot, small paper plates, and plastic forks.

Increase ingredients: Double recipe.

Chapter 3

Gnocchi Potato Pasta: Equipment needed: portable electric burner to cook potatoes and gnocchi in pot, strong plastic forks for eating with and marking gnocchi, paper bowls.

Increase ingredients: Double recipe.

Chapter 4

Babka Easter Yeast Cake: Equipment needed: portable toaster oven, two bundt pans, paper plates, and plastic forks.

Increase ingredients: Make two recipes for two cakes.

Chapter 5

Matzoh Balls and Chicken Soup: Equipment needed: portable electric burner to cook soup and matzoh balls in pot, soup bowls, and spoons.

Increase ingredients: Double the matzoh ball recipe. Do not double chicken soup, but do use smaller servings.

Chapter 6

Portuguese Sweet Bread: Equipment needed: four 9-inch pie plates, portable toaster oven, four cake racks, four dish towels, an extra floured wooden or plastic board, and one more mixing bowl.

Increase ingredients: Make two bread recipes.

Chapter 7

Fried Rice: Equipment needed: electric frying pan, small bowls, and chopsticks.

Increase ingredients: Double recipe.

Chapter 8

Sukiyaki: Equipment needed: two electric griddles, two pairs of tongs, two extra platters, small bowls, and chopsticks.

Increase ingredients: Double recipe.

ACKNOWLEDGEMENTS

I would like to thank Jan Davey Ellis for illustrating my history/cookbooks with such charm and clever artistry.

I also want to thank the many people I consulted with for recipes and cultural information, including Cidália Jordao and her mother, Ilda Figueiredo, both Portuguese immigrants, who gave me invaluable advice on how to make a proper sweetbread. My daughter, Tina Ichord Johansson and her Swedish mother in-law, Anita Johansson, for providing me with a splendid Swedish meatball recipe. My Italian-American cousin, Gloria Leveroni and her gift of wonderful stories and recipes. A sentimental thanks to my Irish-American side of the family, the beloved Duffeys, who cooked all those wonderful meals and left me with the memories. Finally, to the Jewish-Americans and Greek-Americans who answered all my questions at their charming festivals.

SOURCE NOTES

Studying the culinary traditions of the early immigrants who came to America has been truly an education. I found some interesting books on the subject, but the three most helpful and informative were *Coming To America: A History of Immigration and Ethncity in American Life* by Roger Daniels, *The Frugal Gourmet on Our Immigrant Ancestors* by Jeff Smith, and *American Cooking: The Melting Pot*, a Time-Life Book. I referred to these three volumes again and again as I worked my way through this project. They provided the when, why, and where each group settled in America and how their cherished recipes and customs carried them through the tough times.

In each chapter I added to the information from the above books, with facts from other texts, periodicals, and Web sites. In Chapter 1, *American Food: The Gastronomic Story* by Evan Jones was full of information about the food customs of the early Spaniards, French, Dutch, and Swedes who came to the New World. Evan Jones's book was also a great source for Chapter 2 on the German and Irish immigrants along with *The Cooking of the British Isle*s, a Time-Life book, and the *Lancaster County Cookbook* by Louise Stultifies and Jan Mast. In Chapter 3, *The Frugal Gourmet Cooks Italian* by Jeff Smith added in-depth flavor to Italian customs and foods. Chapter 4 took information from many books on the eastern European immigrant experience including a favorite, *Flavors of Hungary* by Charlotte Slovak Biro. The Jewish cooking books, *Jewish Cooking In America*, and *The Children's Jewish Holiday Kitchen* both written by Joan Nathan, led me to understand the complex dietary laws of the Jewish immigrants discussed in Chapter 5. Articles and Web sites gave dimension to the immigrants covered in Chapter 6, including Jennifer Reese's piece in Via magazine, "Festa, Music, Feasting, Parades, And Bullfights Give A Portuguese Flavor To California's Heartland." In Chapters 7 and 8, books by Johnny Kan: *Eight Immortal Flavors: Secrets of Cantonese Cookery in San Francisco's Chinatown*, and *Japanese Cooking Now: The Real Thing* by Joan Itoh added colorful and charming details about the Chinese and Japanese cultures.

In addition to using texts in my research, I also watched several videos produced by the History Channel for background information on several of the ethnic groups discussed in this book. The titles of these videos are: *Ellis Island: The Irish in America* hosted by Aidan Quinn; *Italians In America: The Journey* and *Italians In America: Home*; *Chinatown: Strangers In A Strange Land*.

I also had a chance to taste, see, and learn about the Jewish-American culture at the Jewish Food & Cultural Festival hosted by Congregation Beth Shalom in Modesto, California. Then I stuffed myself with baklava while being charmed by Greek music and dancing at the Greek Food Festival held at the Greek Orthodox Church of the Annunciation in Modesto, California. In addition, I attended a beautiful festa at the Turlock Pentecost Association 92nd Annual Holy Spirit Celebration.

BIBLIOGRAPHY

Adams, Willi Paul. "The German Americans: An Ethnic Experience." Berlin, Germany, 1990. 5/1/2003. *http://www.ulib.iupui.edu/kade/adams/toc.html*

Allan, Tony. *The Irish Famine: The Birth of Irish America.* Chicago: Heinemann Library, 2001.

Bailey, Adrian, and the Editors of Time-Life Books. *The Cooking of the British Isles.* New York: Time-Life Books, 1969.

Biro, Charlotte Slovak. *Flavors of Hungary.* San Ramon, CA: Chevron Chemical Company, 1973.

Daniels, Roger. *Coming To America: A History of Immigration and Ethnicity in American Life.* New York: HarperCollins Publishers, 1990.

Elliott, Vicky. "Blessing the Baskets: Polish Tradition of Easter Eve Alive in San Jose." *San Francisco Chronicle,* April 7, 2002.

Feibleman, Peter S., and the Editors of Time-Life Books. *The Cooking of Spain and Portugal.* New York: Time-Life Books, 1969.

Freedman, Russell. *Immigrant Kids.* New York: Puffin Books, 1980.

"Greek Americans," *Cobblestone: The History Magazine for Young People,* December 1996.

Hébert, Malcolm. "The Creole and Cajun Cooking of Louisiana." 2/12/2003. *http://www.gumbopages.com/food/about-food.html*

ICA Test Kitchen. *Swedish Cooking.* Västerås, Sweden: ICA Bokförlag, 1971.

Itoh, Joan. *Japanese Cooking Now: The Real Thing.* New York: Warner Books, Inc., 1980.

Jann's PA Dutch Kitchen: *Pennsylvania Dutch Cookery.* 1998. 12/30/2002 *http://www.geocities.com/arojann.geo/cookery.html*

"Japanese Americans," *Cobblestone: The History Magazine for Young People,* April 1996.

Jones, Evan. *American Food: The Gastronomic Story.* New York: E.P. Dutton & Co., 1975.

Jones, Wilbert. *Regional American Cuisine:* "Guide to Culinary & Chef Techniques," December 2000 Issue. 3/21/2003. *http://www.preparedfppds.com/archives/2000/2000_12/0012rac1.htm*

Kan, Johnny. *Eight Immortal Flavors: Secrets Of Cantonese Cookery In San Francisco's Chinatown.* San Francisco: California Living Books, 1980.

Nathan, Joan. *Jewish Cooking in America.* New York: Alfred A. Knopf, 1994.

———. *The Children's Jewish Holiday Kitchen.* New York: Schocken Books, 1987.

O'Connor, Kyrie. "How to Eat Chinese Food." *The Modesto Bee,* January 29, 2003.

The Passover on the Net. Studio Melizo, 1995–2000. 3/18/2003. *http://www.holidays.net/passover/index.htm*

Ramerini, Marco. "The Dutch and Swedish Settlements in North America." 2/15/2003.

http://www.geocities.com/Athens/Styx/6497/newnether.html

Reese, Jennifer. "Festa! Music, Feasting, Parades, and Bullfights Give a Portuguese Flavor to California's Heartland." *VIA* magazine, May/June 2003.

Sandler, Martin W. *Immigrants: A Library of Congress Book.* New York: HarperCollins Publishers, 1995.

Shenton, James P., and Angelo M. Pellegrini, and Brown, Dale, and Shenker, Israel, and Wood, Peter, and the Editors of Time-Life Books. *American Cooking: The Melting Pot.* New York: Time-Life Books, 1971.

Siegel, Helene. *The Ethnic Kitchen: French Cooking for Beginners.* New York: HarperCollins Publishers, 1994.

Smith, Jeff. *The Frugal Gourmet on our Immigrant Ancestors.* New York: Avon Books, 1990.

———. *The Frugal Gourmet Cooks Italian.* New York: William Morrow and Company, Inc., 1993.

———. *The Frugal Gourmet Cooks American.* New York: William Morrow and Company, Inc., 1987.

"St. Augustine," *Cobblestone: The History Magazine for Young People,* November 1995.

Steinberg, Rafael, and the Editors of Time-Life Books. *The Cooking of Japan.* New York: Time-Life Books, 1969.

Stepanchuk, Carol. *Exploring Chinatown: A Children's Guide to Chinese Culture.* Berkeley, CA: Pacific View Press, 2002.

Stoltzfus, Louise, and Jan Mast. *Lancaster County Cookbook.* Intercourse, PA: Good Books, 1993.

Wu, Olivia. "Cracking the Code: We Uncover What It Takes to Get Real Regional Chinese Cuisine." *San Francisco Chronicle* magazine, July 7, 2002.

INDEX